21ST-CENTURY ECONOMICS

UNDERSTANDING DEPRESSIONS

CHET'LA SEBREE

Cavendish
Square
New York

Published in 2020 by Cavendish Square Publishing, LLC
243 5th Avenue, Suite 136, New York, NY 10016

Library of Congress Cataloging-in-Publication Data

Names: Sebree, Chet'la, author.
Title: Understanding economic depressions / Chet'la Sebree.
Description: First Edition. | New York : Cavendish Square, [2018] |
Series: 21st-century economics | Audience: Grades 7-12. |
Includes bibliographical references and index.
Identifiers: LCCN 2018045340 (print) | LCCN 2018047143 (ebook) |
ISBN 9781502645951 (ebook) | ISBN 9781502645944 (library bound) |
ISBN 9781502645937 (pbk.)
Subjects: LCSH: Depressions--Juvenile literature.
Classification: LCC HB3711 (ebook) | LCC HB3711 .S437 2018 (print) |
DDC 338.5/42--dc23
LC record available at https://lccn.loc.gov/2018045340

Editorial Director: David McNamara
Copy Editor: Nathan Heidelberger
Associate Art Director: Alan Sliwinski
Designer: Jessica Nevins
Production Coordinator: Karol Szymczuk
Photo Research: J8 Media

Portions of this book originally appeared in *How a Depression Works* by Jason Porterfield.

The photographs in this book are used by permission and through the courtesy of: Cover Everett Collection/Shutterstock.com; p. 4, 22, 54 Bettmann/Getty Images; p. 7 FPG/Hulton Archive/Getty Images; p. 8 Scott Dalton/Bloomberg/Getty Images; p. 10 Dorothea Lange/Library of Congress; p. 14 Lili White/Shutterstock.com; p. 15 GHI/UIG/ Getty Images; p. 18 Qilai Shen/Bloomberg/Getty Images; p. 20 Stock Montage/Getty Images; p. 21 Mandritoiu/Shutterstock.com; p. 24 Siraanamwong/iStockphoto.com; p. 27 Sirtravelalot/Shutterstock.com; p. 28 Library of Congress/Corbis/VCG/Getty Images; p. 31 DEA/Biblioteca Ambrosiana/Getty Images; p. 32 Dorothea Lange/PhotoQuest/ Getty Images; p. 36 Zentilia/Shutterstock.com; p. 40-41 Milos Bicanski/Getty images; p. 42, 62-63 Corbis/Getty Images; p. 44 Photo/Diego Giudice/AP Images; p. 48 Michael Norcia/Sygma/Getty Images; p. 56 Louisa Gouliamaki/AFP/Getty Images; p. 58 Jose Luis Pelaez Inc./Blend Images/ Getty Images; p. 67 Evan ElAmin/Shutterstock.com.

Printed in the United States of America

CONTENTS

ECONOMIC DEPRESSIONS

In 2008, a financial crisis rattled global economies. People were losing their jobs, and many of them were unable to find new work. At the same time, prices were increasing for food, gas, and other goods. Many people who borrowed money to buy a home or make other large purchases in earlier years when cash and credit were flowing freely were now struggling to pay their mortgages and other debts. Even some banks, unable to collect on the loans they had issued, were having trouble staying open. This financial crisis, often called the Great Recession, was small in comparison to the Great Depression of the twentieth century.

Opposite: People flooded New York City streets when the stock market crashed in October 1929. This marked the beginning of the Great Depression.

Changes in the Economy

Economies are constantly changing. Employment, wages, and production are in a constant state of flux. National economies can go through many different stages as they react to changing conditions. For example, inflation is the general increase in the cost of goods and services for the average person. Bubbles occur when part of the economy appears healthier than it really is, while booms are the rapid growth of parts of the economy.

Generally, the economy may go through a period of incredible growth for a year or two before leveling off. The economy may stagnate, or remain relatively unchanged, and then be followed by another period of growth. It may even fall into a recession or depression. Recessions happen when the economy slows for a period of time because fewer people are buying goods and services, and fewer people have jobs. Extremely long or severe recessions are called depressions.

Depressions and Recessions

An economic depression is defined as a period during which business, employment, and stock values decline severely or remain at a very low level of activity. Although some people believe depressions are a part of normal economic cycles, they are not. Economists are used to seeing ups and downs in the economy as part of a

During the Great Depression, people waited in line
for everything from food to potential jobs.

continuous cycle of ups and downs. However, depressions
are much more severe than the ordinary downturns that
economists expect.

Recessions are usually brief economic downturns that
occur when the value of a nation's goods and services
declines. Marked by increased unemployment, stagnant
wages, and falling retail sales, a recession generally is

During the Great Recession, people also found themselves waiting in line. Here, people wait in line for a job fair at the Toyota Center in Houston, Texas.

much milder than a depression. The end of a recession is usually signaled by rising employment levels and greater spending by consumers.

If a recession lasts a very long time and keeps getting worse, it could turn into a depression. Depressions are recessions marked by very sharp, severe drops in business activity, employment, and the stock market.

While economies usually come out of recessions within a year or two, depressions can last much longer. Depressions also affect a broader range of people than a recession does. A large percentage of the population struggles with economic hardship and inflation. Often, depressions have an international effect. The most recent economic depression in the United States was the Great Depression. It started in 1929 after the stock market crashed and lasted through the 1930s. It had a worldwide effect. While the United States eventually came out of the Great Depression, the memory of hard times lasted for decades. In fact, the Great Depression helped reshape the country's economic policies and institutions, many of which are still in place today.

CHAPTER 1

THE ECONOMY

Economists explain the ups and downs of the economy as simply being a part of the business cycle. Business cycles are made up of four phases: peak, contraction (or recession), trough, and expansion (or recovery). Economists cannot predict the exact phases of a cycle or say how long they may last. However, the economy is always in one of these four phases. When shown on a graph, these phases look like a roller coaster. The cycle begins with a peak, when the economy is doing well. It drops when the markets contract, or shrink, until the market hits a trough, or a low point. After that, the economy starts climbing again, expanding and recovering. Eventually, the economy will hit another peak, and the cycle will start again.

Opposite: Depressions are not a part of the normal business cycle. They make it difficult for families to afford basic necessities.

The Four Phases of the Business Cycle

Peaks occur when the economy is performing near its highest possible level. This usually means unemployment is low, which indicates that companies can afford to hire and pay people. Similarly, peaks occur when the gross domestic product (GDP), or the total market value of goods and services produced by workers and capital

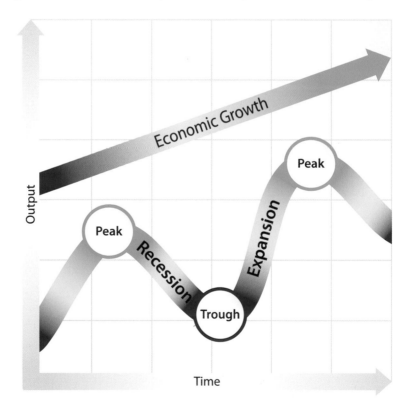

The business cycle goes through several phases: peak, recession (or contraction), trough, and expansion (or recovery). The length of each phase changes each time.

within a nation's borders during a given period, is rising. In a peak, the GDP has reached a high.

The peak ends when the economy starts to contract. This contraction period, also known as a recession, is a downturn in the business cycle. The GDP and corporate profits decline during this economic downturn. Meanwhile, unemployment goes up. Ultimately, the economy will reach a point where unemployment stops increasing and economic output stops decreasing. This point is the trough. It is the third stage and the bottom of the business cycle. The length of time between the peak and the trough marks how long the recession has lasted.

The trough represents both good and bad news for the economy. On the one hand, it represents the economy's worst conditions. On the other hand, a trough also marks the beginning of the last phase of the business cycle, the recovery period, where the markets will begin to expand again toward a peak. Companies start hiring again, and people begin spending more money. Production is increased to meet this rising demand, resulting in more hiring and more consumer spending. A positive cycle begins and gathers momentum. The economy may even enter a boom period, in which it grows very rapidly. The economy begins working its way to another peak, at which point the business cycle starts over again.

The Difference Between Depressions and Recessions

The words "depression" and "recession" both describe economic downturns, and it isn't always clear how they are different. A depression is a rare but extreme form of recession. Lenders stop offering people credit and loans. Fewer people invest their money in the stock market, and the value of money itself goes down. Prices fall as demand for goods evaporates. People's assets, such as their homes, lose value.

Depressions are primarily marked, however, by a major and long-lasting shortfall in consumers' ability to buy goods and services, compared with the economy's potential ability to produce them. During a depression, unemployment may increase dramatically because companies can no longer afford to pay or hire workers if no one is buying their goods.

The economy gets stuck in this cycle because vast numbers of people without jobs and assets cannot afford to boost the economy, which means companies cannot afford to offer more opportunities. It often takes years and dramatic change like outside events for an economy to climb out of a depression. For instance, the US economy didn't bounce back from the Great Depression until the country joined the war effort to produce goods for countries fighting in World War II.

During World War II, women worked in factories for companies like Buick, which focused on aircraft motors during the war.

Government intervention can also lift a country out of a depression. This intervention can take the form of large public spending, building projects, and cash bailouts of struggling industries. It can also include taxpayer relief in the form of tax cuts and refunds. The government can also get involved by setting a lower interest rate, or the amount of extra money that needs to be paid back when someone takes out a loan.

Economic Indicators

Today, experts use statistics and data called economic indicators to judge the economy's performance. The unemployment rate is one such indicator. The unemployment rate measures the number of people who do not have jobs but are looking for work. A low unemployment rate shows that companies are doing well and hiring workers. A rising unemployment rate often means that some companies are firing workers while others are simply not hiring. This can be a strong sign that the economy is weakening. Inflation is another indicator. It refers to the rising cost of goods and services over a period of time. It can also signal a decreased value of money. In both cases, goods and services become more expensive. This is either because their sticker prices are rising or because the dollar is worth less than it used to be, meaning it buys less than it did before the inflationary period began.

Economists generally agree that inflation happens when the money supply grows faster than the economy grows. There is too much money in circulation in the economy, perhaps due to easy loans, credit, and rising wages. When there is a lot of money in circulation, its value—its actual purchasing power—decreases. Inflation can also happen when there's an underproduction of goods and services that are in demand. When products are in demand but the supply is low, companies can charge more because people will pay higher prices to get their hands on them.

Gross Domestic Product and Gross National Product

Two of the most important economic indicators are numbers called the gross domestic product (GDP) and the gross national product (GNP). The GNP is the market value, or the amount for which something can be sold, of all goods and services made using resources owned by people and companies from a particular country. These resources can include materials, stores, or factories that are located in other countries. So, an American-based company that sells clothing in France made from Chinese silk and manufactured in Indian factories contributes to the GNP of the United States.

The GDP represents a part of the GNP. The GDP stands for the total value of all goods and services at current market prices produced within a country within a given year. In this case, the goods and services must be

The products made at this Ford Motor Company plant in China contribute to the United States' gross national product, or GNP, but not to its gross domestic product, or GDP.

produced on American soil in order for them to contribute to the United States' GDP.

Both the GDP and the GNP are important numbers for economists because they reflect the health of the economy. If these numbers go up over a period of time, it means that the economy is generally strong—businesses are effectively producing and selling products. If the GDP and GNP's rates of increase slow, they reveal that the growth of the economy itself is slowing. This means there may be trouble on the way. A drop in these numbers may signal a recession. If the GDP drops by more than 10 percent, it usually signals the beginning of a depression. For instance, the GDP in the United States only dropped 4.3 percent during the Great Recession. It dropped nearly 30 percent during the Great Depression.

US DEPARTMENT OF THE TREASURY

In the United States, the president is responsible for the economy; however, he seeks advice from the US Department of the Treasury. Congress created the department in 1789 to manage and protect government finances. Alexander Hamilton, statesman and Founding Father, was the first secretary of the treasury, the person responsible for running the department. He believed in the US economy and helped the country recover from its national debt after the American Revolution.

Hamilton circa 1790.

Generally, the Department of the Treasury is responsible for ensuring the strength of the economy, creating employment opportunities, and supporting economic prosperity, or positive growth. The department does this through advising the president, properly regulating financial institutions, and borrowing the money necessary to keep the US government operational. It does this work with the help of other US government agencies, foreign governments, and global financial institutions. Additionally, it oversees the production of currency.

The department must also ensure national security through the protection of the US economy from threats abroad. In the twenty-first century, this means that the department must protect against cyber attacks on the economy. A number of chief investment strategists at major investment firms like Charles Schwab have stated that a cyber attack on a major financial institution could trigger the next financial crisis, causing panic from investors and a drop in stock prices. This is a concern because of how large and technologically dependent the financial industry is in the twenty-first century. The Department of the Treasury is responsible for safeguarding against these threats.

The Department of the Treasury has been housed in the same building in Washington, DC, since the mid-nineteenth century.

CHAPTER 2

THE ROOTS OF A DEPRESSION

Often it seems like depressions are triggered by one big event, like a major industry collapse that puts thousands of people out of work. For many years, people thought the Great Depression was caused by the stock market crash of 1929. However, depressions occur when other economic issues have been festering under the surface for months or years. For instance, the Great Depression had many causes, including overspeculation, or the belief that stocks would earn more than they could, and underconsumption, or people buying far fewer goods than companies were producing.

Opposite: The Great Depression affected both the wealthy and the poor. For instance, some stockbrokers lost all of their money in the 1929 crash and were forced to sell anything they could.

Price Fluctuations and Their Effect

Prices for goods and services rise and fall over time. Economists call these changes fluctuations. Local fluctuations are price changes for goods that are sold in their country of origin. International price fluctuations happen to goods that are exported and sold in other countries.

Often, price fluctuations follow the law of supply and demand. Prices rise when there is a shortage or if a

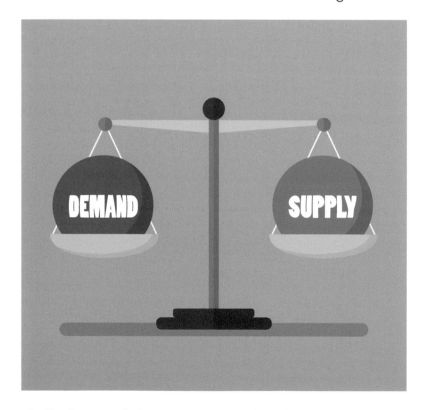

Ideally, there is a balance between supply and demand. Price is a major factor in achieving this balance.

product is new. Prices fall when the market is flooded with a product or service, as companies compete for customers who have a wide range of choices. Many companies export goods to sell in other countries. These companies can make large profits if there's not already a similar product for sale on the foreign market and the demand is high. However, if the demand weakens, it may no longer be worthwhile to spend the money to ship a product overseas.

The change in prices over time is measured by the consumer price index (CPI). This index averages the change in prices for consumer goods and services over time. It tracks things like the price of electricity, gas, and food over a specific period. In the years leading up to the Great Depression, there was a period of sharp inflation. Between 1913 and 1929, the CPI increased by 72.7 percent. That is an average of a 3.5 percent annual increase in prices for certain goods.

This sort of rapid inflation can trigger a depression. As prices for goods rise, they can exceed what people are willing or able to pay for said goods. Sometimes this inability or unwillingness is coupled with the decrease in the value of money because of the inflation. This can lead to a further inability to pay for consumer goods. When people can no longer afford products, stores and businesses have to cut jobs or close to recover from the loss of profit when the cost to produce goods outweighs the amount for which the goods are sold.

Conversely, between 1929 and 1941, the CPI decreased by 14 percent, averaging to an annual decrease in the price for goods of about 1.3 percent. This decrease in prices during the Great Depression allowed for people to better afford consumer goods. However, it didn't necessarily make it easier for businesses to prosper on the reduced rates of their products.

Both local and international price fluctuations can impact a nation's economy. Local fluctuations affect the ability of people to buy goods and services. They also affect the ability of business owners to make a profit. During recessions and depressions, people often cut back on buying things they don't really need. Businesses often lower prices to attract increasingly scarce buyers. Although charging less may attract some customers, it also reduces profits.

Price fluctuations also affect the job market. If fewer people are buying a company's products, prices fall and profits decrease. As a result, the company may cut its workforce. For instance, many companies severely cut production during the Great Depression. Unemployment rose because of these production cuts. By cutting production, companies saved money they would have otherwise spent on raw materials and labor. However,

When demand for a product is low, companies will often offer discounts in order to encourage consumers to purchase their supply.

they also limited the number of their products available for sale to consumers, which limited their profits.

Other Factors

Natural disasters and wars also play a role in depressions. For instance, many of the depressions in the United States during the nineteenth century were caused by droughts or crop failures. During the Great Depression, dry conditions

Dust storms caused massive agricultural damage in the 1930s.

and wind storms in the central plains region of the United States led to the Dust Bowl, during which people could not farm on their destroyed land.

Wars can help bring on depressions when fighting destroys factories, farmland, and materials. Countries at war may have to borrow money from other countries to pay for the expenses of continued fighting. Repaying the debt can severely stress a nation already battered by war. Ironically, however, wars can also help end depressions by putting people to work making things like weapons, armored vehicles, aircrafts, ships, and uniforms.

Events taking place in other parts of the world can also help cause depressions. During the 1920s, much of Europe was still recovering from World War I. Factories in many European countries had been damaged by the war, and these countries had to import goods from the United States in order to rebuild. The United States profited greatly from this trade imbalance at first. However, when European economies collapsed, American companies lost much of their export business.

NINETEENTH-CENTURY DEPRESSIONS

During the nineteenth century, five major financial panics hit the United States: in 1819, 1837, 1857, 1873, and 1893. All five led to what were then called depressions. The Panic of 1819 resulted in the first depression in US history. The economy had been struggling since the United States went to war with Great Britain in the War of 1812 (1812–1815). At the time, cotton was one of the country's biggest exports and a key part of the economy. Cotton prices fell sharply in 1819. This dramatic shift in the economy caused banks and lenders to ask people to repay their loans. As a result, farms were foreclosed, or taken over by the banks that farmers owed money to. Many banks also collapsed during the panic. It lasted until 1821.

Several factors caused the Panic of 1837. Cotton prices collapsed again, and wheat crops failed. Land speculation, in which people rapidly purchased and sold overvalued land in hopes of making a profit, resulted in a burst real estate bubble and the loss of investments. At the time, many states issued their own currency, which caused confusion and inflation. Many financial firms in New York City and state-sponsored banks failed, and the cost of labor dropped sharply, along with real estate and food prices. The panic, which lasted six years, is the second longest in US history.

The Panic of 1893 was the worst panic in the United States' history until the Great Depression. The stock market dropped that spring and then crashed in June, as panicked stockholders sold off their shares. By the end of the year, more than sixteen thousand businesses had failed. Among the failed businesses were over one hundred railroads and nearly five hundred banks. Unemployment climbed until one in six Americans was unemployed. The panic finally ended in 1897.

Prior to the Great Depression of the 1930s, the Panic of 1873 was regarded as a great depression.

CHAPTER 3

LIFE DURING A DEPRESSION

People often have to make serious sacrifices during a depression. Families cut their spending on all but the most necessary goods. Today, families would likely cut back on cell phone data plans, cable, vacations, clothes, and toys. They may drive less or get rid of their second car in order to save money on gas, repairs, and insurance. Families may also sell their prized possessions like homes, boats, jewelry, or family heirlooms to make ends meet. If a parent's wages or hours are cut or if a family member loses his or her job, younger family members may get a job.

Opposite: It was not uncommon for children to work to support their families during the Great Depression.

The Realities of Unemployment

A rising unemployment rate reveals that businesses are not only not hiring new workers but are in fact cutting their workforce. The effects of rising unemployment can be far reaching. A higher unemployment rate means that more workers are jobless and looking for employment. Without their paychecks, they have very little to spend. Even workers who still have their jobs contribute to the continued slump. They may save more of their money rather than spending it, fearful that they, too, will soon lose their jobs. During depressions, unemployment may reach into the double digits. During the Great Depression, unemployment peaked at around 25 percent in 1933, which meant that one out of every four American workers was out of a job.

Bankruptcy and Debt Management

In a depression, creditors—institutions or individuals who loan money—often call in their debts in an effort to keep money moving in and out of the institution smoothly. With the economy suffering, a debtor, whether it be a business or an individual, may not be able to afford to pay off loans and may be forced to declare bankruptcy. When a person or an organization files for bankruptcy, that person or organization is legally declaring an inability to pay back creditors.

Declaring bankruptcy is actually a good way to assure creditors that they will be paid eventually. It gives them and the debtor an opportunity to come up with a realistic repayment schedule that will satisfy the lenders and give the debtors some extra time and breathing room. In a worst-case scenario, the person or business owner may have to sell off assets like real estate, office equipment, or even a business itself to pay the debts.

Bankruptcy does not wipe away debt or free an individual from repaying it. It simply gives a person or a business more time to do so and may reduce the amount owed. The drawback is the person or business that declared bankruptcy will be considered much less credit-worthy in the future and will probably have trouble obtaining additional loans, mortgages, and credit cards.

Decreased Credit

Credit problems are another factor that can both signal the beginning of an economic slump and contribute further to the downturn. Before the Great Depression began, people freely borrowed money in order to purchase homes and new and expensive technological wonders, such as automobiles, refrigerators, and radios. At the time, banks and other creditors had the fluidity to make these loans because cash was flowing freely throughout the expanding economy. But when the stock market

People use credit cards to purchase goods and services when they don't immediately have access to cash.

collapsed and creditors started calling in loans, many people couldn't pay them back. Banks collapsed, and bankers became much less willing to risk lending money.

The restricted credit during the Great Depression harmed the economy in several ways. People could no longer borrow money in order to purchase goods, nor could they borrow money to help pay off their other debts. Businesses also had a much harder time borrowing money. Businesses often rely on short-term loans in order to pay workers and buy supplies and materials. They use their product stock as a guarantee that they can pay the loan. For example, a store may use the value of its merchandise as a guarantee or proof that it can repay the loan it is asking for. But if businesses can't borrow money, they can't pay workers or purchase materials for the manufacture of their products, and business grinds to a halt. The halt in production leads to a drop in stock value, which tends to deepen the slump.

More on Price Fluctuations

Prices for goods generally tend to drop during depressions. This sounds like good news, as it would make it easier for people with little money to make purchases. However, it actually spells trouble for the economy. Sellers are forced to lower prices on their goods to attract buyers. They may have to drop prices to the point where they are forced to sell their products for less than it costs to produce them. If they keep losing money this way, businesses may eventually be forced to close, triggering greater unemployment.

There's also the chance that some goods could actually go up in price, even during a depression. Business owners who make or sell a product that's in high demand may take advantage of the situation by raising prices, especially if that product is considered essential, such as bread, eggs, meat, or fuel.

Overall, though, price fluctuations during a depression usually mean lower wages and lower values for homes. Unfortunately, one thing that does not drop is the amount

QUICK Q&A

Are depressions part of normal business cycles?
No. While contraction periods, or recessions, are part of the normal business cycle, depressions are extremely severe economic downturns from which an economy can take years to recover.

Can one major event cause a depression?
Not likely. Although some depressions are triggered by one main event, like when the collapse of the Ohio Life Insurance and Trust Company triggered the Panic of 1857, often depressions are the result of much larger issues within the economy, like overspeculation and inflation.

Does a country's depression only affect its own economy?
Not usually. Global economies are closely linked through international trade, and serious problems in one country can often set off trouble around the world.

What can we do to avoid another depression?
In most countries, citizens entrust the federal government with the nation's financial health. The government must do things like contain inflation, manage interest rates, and encourage strong international trade relationships.

of debt that a person owes on loans to banks or credit card companies.

Social Unrest

Depressions are often marked by social unrest, and sometimes major changes take place in society as a result. During these times, people feel frightened and insecure. They may be angry at the government for mishandling the economy or resent the wealthy who don't share their hardships. For instance, when Argentina found itself in deep financial crisis in the early twenty-first century, the country went through five presidents in two weeks. This was after riots broke out in the capital of Buenos Aires. Citizens were expressing their frustration with food scarcity and the high unemployment rate, which neared the US unemployment rate during the Great Depression.

In past depressions, riots have been common responses to shortages, unemployment, or government policies. In the midst of Greece's financial crisis in the early twenty-first century, citizens rioted against austerity measures. These measures are government actions taken to cut spending and increase revenue. The unemployed may march, as veterans did in the United States during the Great Depression to petition for a bonus they were

In February 2010, Greeks marched to protest the government's plan to curb spending and reduce national debt.

promised for their service in World War I. These types of demonstrations have often led to clashes with the police that result in injury or death.

Crime in general usually rises during depressions. Desperate people may go outside of the law in order to make money or obtain food, robbing banks, committing burglaries, or shoplifting. Violent crimes may also increase. Between 2014 and 2017, still in the thick of Greece's financial crisis, there were nearly fourteen thousand reported domestic violence cases, with women making up 70 percent of the victims. In a similar vein, during the Great Depression, bank robbers like John Dillinger

African Americans who continued to work throughout
the Great Depression often worked in segregated units,
or groups that were separate from white workers.

and the famous duo of Bonnie Parker and Clyde Barrow
captured the public's imagination by robbing the banks
that some people blamed for causing the depression and
seizing their homes, farms, or savings.

More Burdens to Bear

On top of debt and financial stress, many people also face prejudice during depressions. For instance, African Americans had faced discrimination in the United States long before the Great Depression began. As the depression grew worse, however, working African Americans were often laid off from their jobs so that those jobs could be given to white workers. About 50 percent of African American workers were unemployed by 1932, compared to the 25 percent of white workers who were unemployed.

Similar racial tensions have erupted in Greece during its financial crisis. In the midst of social unrest in countries like Syria, illegal immigration to Greece has skyrocketed. The financially unstable country's citizens, as well as neo-Nazi groups like the Golden Dawn, have targeted people they perceive might be undocumented immigrants. In 2013, the US Embassy in Greece noted that Americans who were of African, Asian, Hispanic, or Middle Eastern descent were at risk of "unprovoked harassment and violent attacks" in major cities like Athens.

As financial uncertainty deepens in a country, it is not uncommon for other tensions to rise.

CHAPTER 4

GLOBAL FINANCIAL CRISIS

S everal countries have experienced severe financial crises in the twenty-first century. For instance, at the turn of the century, Argentina faced a sustained recession. The contraction period lasted several years, during which the nation's debt reached about 150 percent of the country's GDP. Similarly, it took Greece much longer to pull itself out of the financial crisis after the Great Recession than it did for other countries in the European Union. Although the Great Recession was felt worldwide, it did not carry the same magnitude as the Great Depression—the most recent global depression to date.

Opposite: Soup kitchens fed hundreds of children during Argentina's financial crisis.

The First Years of the Great Depression

Although people started to feel the effects of the Great Depression after the stock market crash of 1929, it took a few years for the reality of the vast depths of the depression to set in. Even as the depression deepened in 1930, the situation didn't seem any worse to some Americans than it had been during the last financial crisis. Just before the economic boom of the 1920s began, the country had suffered through a recession that lasted from 1920 to 1921, with the unemployment rate rising above 10 percent. By the end of 1930, the unemployment rate had not reached 9 percent yet.

In the fall of 1930, President Herbert Hoover formed a committee called the President's Emergency Committee for Employment in an attempt to end the crisis. The organization did very little to help the situation. It failed to gather any real statistics on the economic crisis or organize any relief efforts. Instead, it focused mostly on trying to restore the public's confidence in the economy. President Hoover and his government opposed federal relief efforts. Hoover believed in rugged individualism, the concept that people can help themselves without government intervention.

With the federal government checked out, local and state governments were left to pick up the slack and deal with the needs of the growing number of unemployed people. By 1932, these governments had run out of funds. Raising state taxes was not an option, since many citizens would be unwilling or unable to pay. Many states also had laws forbidding their governments from operating with unbalanced budgets, meaning that they couldn't spend more than they took in. In 1932, only a handful of states offered any sort of relief payments to unemployed workers.

The Gold Standard

When the Great Depression first began in 1929, the value of the US dollar was directly linked to the value of gold. This gold standard meant that people could take their paper money or bonds into a bank and have it redeemed for an equivalent amount of actual gold. Many of the world's economies at the time were based on the gold standard. The value of gold linked these economies together.

One problem with the gold standard was that it made the money supply very rigid. If governments printed money beyond the value of the gold held in banks, the money would lose value because it couldn't be redeemed for the same amount of gold. If people started to hoard money during these times when it became less valuable, waiting for its value to increase again, there would be a physical shortage of cash available. The gold standard

Even though the United States no longer uses the gold standard, some banks still have gold stored in their vaults.

also linked world economies closely together based on the global value of gold. Cash shortages in one country could affect the value of gold worldwide. Likewise, the number of people trading in their cash for gold would also affect its value.

After a wave of bank failures in some parts of Europe, problems soon spread to Great Britain, as worried people pulled their money out of British banks. The British pound was one of the most important currencies in the world and was linked to the value of many other nations' currencies. But people afraid of a bank collapse sought the safety of actual, physical wealth (rather than paper currency) and withdrew their gold from banks in large numbers. As a result, the pound lost value, and Great Britain was forced to stop using the gold standard in September 1931.

Bank Failures and a Balance Budget

When Great Britain went off the gold standard, many other countries were also forced to abandon it. In the United States, however, the Federal Reserve, a government agency that acts as the country's central bank, moved to keep the gold standard. The Federal Reserve had to cut the money supply—the amount of money in circulation. They needed to reduce the money supply so that the amount of money in circulation would equal the amount of gold US banks held in reserve. One way to take excess currency out of circulation was to raise interest rates on loans. This made it more expensive for people to borrow money, so soon less money was in circulation. This led to deflation—scarcity of cash, decreased purchasing, a wholesale drop in prices, and a drop in production.

As banks called in loans, customers postponed buying things until they had more cash. They also waited to make purchases in the hopes that prices would eventually go down. However, the fall in production led to layoffs, higher unemployment, and even less spending. In many cases, banks had to foreclose on homes because people couldn't pay their debts. As news and rumors spread about banks struggling because of loans not being repaid, depositors began to withdraw their money, fearing that their savings would be lost if the bank failed. This led to even more bank collapses. More than five hundred US banks failed in just the first month after Britain went off the gold standard. By the end of 1931, over two thousand banks failed in the United States, and unemployment had risen to 15.9 percent.

The country faced economic problems far worse than anything it had ever faced before. The federal budget went into a severe deficit. A deficit means that the government is spending more money than it is receiving in a given period of time, such as a year.

Today, it is common for the government to continue spending money, even when there is a budget deficit. But at the time of the Great Depression, balancing the budget seemed like an important first step in fixing the economy. In late 1931, President Hoover asked Congress to pass a tax increase in order to restore balance. The higher taxes placed an even greater burden on people who were out of work, as well as those who were still employed but were struggling with lower wages and devalued currency.

Tariff Trouble

After World War I, the United States profited greatly from selling goods to a war-ravaged Europe. At the same time, the US government had imposed high tariffs on foreign goods. Tariffs are taxes placed on products imported from other countries. They are often meant to protect domestic businesses by making goods from overseas more expensive for people to buy.

In 1927, a world economic conference had ended with many governments agreeing to stop imposing tariffs on foreign goods. The idea was that global trade would improve if there were fewer tariffs, and as a result, the global economy would experience healthy growth.

Many business and government leaders in the United States, however, still supported tariffs. They felt that tariffs protected domestic companies by making their products more competitive. After the stock market crash of 1929, business leaders in the United States pushed the government to set another tariff, despite the 1927 agreement. The result was a tariff bill called the Smoot-Hawley Tariff Act, passed in 1930. Hoover had originally meant for the tariff to help protect farmers, but it had the opposite effect.

Other nations resented the new tariff. Many of these countries owed money to the United States and couldn't hope to pay their debts unless they could sell their products to American consumers. The United States was one of the largest foreign markets at that time. In retaliation, European countries passed their own tariff laws against the United States. As a consequence of the new global tariffs, global trade fell sharply. This made it harder for manufacturers, farmers, and others to sell their goods overseas, and it made the depression worse for people all around the world.

Twenty-First Century Depression

Although there hasn't been a depression in the twenty-first century so far, the Great Recession did have a worldwide effect. It started, however, in the United States. From 2003 to 2006, some sectors of the US economy grew rapidly. Low interest rates and high-risk lending practices made it easy for people to borrow money. This caused an influx of spending, especially in the housing market. House prices rose, and people kept building new houses. However, the economy began slowing in late 2006. Home sales dropped, and so did new home construction. People who had built the new homes and businesses that had supplied building materials soon found that they had much less work than before. Despite the slump, the stock market kept rising, hitting an all-time high that year.

Yet even the markets eventually dropped as bad news started coming in. Creditors lost money as people defaulted on their loans, meaning they could not pay them back. In August 2008, unemployment rose to a five-year high of 6.1 percent, and credit tightened again. As the housing market collapsed, financial markets dropped, and unemployment rose, the government stepped in to try to save banks and businesses. Many credit the lessons learned from the Great Depression with keeping the Great Recession from becoming as devastating. Even still, the effects of this crisis were felt worldwide.

Internationally, European countries were the ones most impacted by the Great Recession because of their close financial and trade relations with the United States. Many of these countries saw a brief recession alongside the United States; however, Greece, in particular, struggled for

DEPRESSION REALITIES

Life for many Americans changed drastically during the Great Depression. Many were out of work and struggled to buy food and other necessities. Many people had a hard time finding enough to eat. One study conducted at the time found that families with at least one fully employed member had 66 percent less illness than families in which

Small shack towns called Hoovervilles sprang up across the country during the Great Depression.

no one was working because they were likely to receive more regular nourishment. Some people living in rural areas sometimes ate weeds to survive. People living in cities sometimes had to dig through garbage cans and city dumps for food.

As unemployment grew, many men started traveling in search of work, sometimes hopping trains to cover greater distances. By 1932, men dressed in battered clothing and seeking work were common sights in many cities and towns. Often, these wandering men were discriminated against by people who thought they were trying to take jobs from working people in the town. At worst, they were seen as potentially dangerous drifters or even classified by local laws as vagrants subject to arrest and imprisonment. Settlements of unemployed men and impoverished, homeless families living in crude shacks—called "Hoovervilles" after President Hoover—cropped up at the edges of towns and cities.

Getting almost no government help from the Hoover administration, charities in some cities and towns set up programs to attempt to feed the growing number of hungry and homeless people. Even still, the struggle continued.

In an act of protest, Greek farmers distributed free fruits and vegetables during the financial crisis.

a prolonged period. Between 2007 and 2013, Greece's GDP fell by 26 percent, meaning that the country was producing less for less value. This decline in GDP was the same as the United States' decline in GDP between 1929 and 1933, the height of the Great Depression. In 2013, Greece's unemployment rate surpassed the highest unemployment rate in the United States during the Great Depression, reaching 28 percent.

In 2018, Greece finally started to climb out of the financial crisis that began in 2008, as it was finally ending its dependence on the nearly $360 billion it was given in bailout money. It received these emergency funds from the European Union and the International Monetary Fund, a specialized international agency of the United Nations responsible for stabilizing economies and facilitating trade. It will still take years, however, for the country's economy to recover from the prolonged devastation.

Although the language of recession has largely been used to describe Greece's financial issues, perhaps in the future it will be seen as a depression because of its sustained, though localized, effect.

CHAPTER 5

CRISIS MANAGEMENT AND RECOVERY

Each economic crisis is unique, with unique causes and resolutions. There is still no single formula for coming out of a depression. Recoveries are dependent upon a number of different factors coming together at the same time.

Policies and Programs to Avoid Depressions

One important step in helping the economy recover is to set relief programs in place to assist those in need. Relief programs may be relatively simple programs that distribute food or clothing to people in need. They may also be complex employment programs designed to find jobs for people who need work.

Opposite: In a healthy economy, people can afford to buy what they need in addition to what they want.

To bring the economy out of a slump, the government often makes policy changes designed to help businesses increase productivity and hire workers. The Federal Reserve System often lowers interest rates during a slump. The lower interest rates encourage borrowing and make it easier for individuals and businesses to repay lenders. Lowering taxes also lessens the tax burden on people and businesses. Money that they would ordinarily have spent on taxes can then be spent in other ways. Consumers can buy products, while businesses can increase production. This spending stimulates the economy and helps it climb out of the trough.

Tax refunds are another tool the government uses to encourage spending. With refunds, taxpayers are given a check from the Internal Revenue Service for a fixed amount. When the housing bubble burst in 2007, foreshadowing the Great Recession, the government responded by issuing tax refunds to everyone who filled out tax forms for the year 2007. Even people who did not have to pay any taxes for the year could receive a refund so long as they filled out the form.

In order to keep people employed during an economic slump, the government may also bail out struggling businesses that employ large numbers of workers. These bailouts, often used for large manufacturers like automakers, can come in the form of management help, loans, and subsidies, or government grants used to assist a company it considers important to the public. Herbert Hoover bailed out some investors during the Great Depression. Similar action was taken in the fall of 2008, as the government approved a $700 billion package to help banks recover from bad mortgage loans. In fact, the government took several cues from Depression-era policies to avoid falling into another depression.

Depression-Era Policies and Programs

President Franklin Roosevelt faced a daunting task when he took office in 1933. The nation's economy was in ruins. People across the country were disheartened. During his inauguration speech, Roosevelt hoped to reassure the country by announcing that "the only thing we have to fear is fear itself."

Roosevelt immediately set to work on the New Deal, a massive series of federal programs and agencies designed to counteract the effects of the Great Depression. One of the goals of the New Deal was to lower production of crops and products to meet the low demand of consumers. Another goal was to increase consumer demand in part by supplying jobs to people through public works

The Civilian Conservation Corps, pictured here, was a New Deal program that put thousands of men to work.

projects. With people earning money by building roads, dams, and schools for the government, they once again had money to spend on goods and services.

Congress passed a series of laws and acts protecting the economy during Roosevelt's first term as president. A law called the Glass-Steagall Act set tougher rules for banks. It also provided insurance to depositors through a new agency called the Federal Deposit Insurance Corporation (FDIC). Even today, this agency guarantees that people will not lose all of their money in the event of a bank collapse.

Other programs developed during this time frame provided direct assistance to people in need. Several bills were passed to help farmers and homeowners pay their mortgages. The Federal Emergency Relief Agency provided grants to states that helped more than twenty

A FEW MORE FACTS

- Unemployment is a strong economic indicator of an economy's financial health. It not only articulates how well businesses are doing by depicting their ability to hire and pay employees, but it also indicates people's ability to spend money on goods and services. The highest rate of unemployment in US history was in 1933.

- Economic depressions are recessions marked by a steep decrease in economic prosperity or a period of stagnation. The last depression to effect global markets was the Great Depression, which lasted from 1929 through the 1930s.

- Until the Great Depression, all economic downturns were called depressions. Economists started using the word "recession" after the Great Depression in order to differentiate between normal downturns and severe crises.

- The worst years of the Great Depression were 1932 and 1933. In 1932, although President Herbert Hoover ran for reelection, he was defeated by Franklin Delano Roosevelt, who took office the next year. Roosevelt was elected to four consecutive terms—more than any other president in US history.

million people get jobs and improve the quality of their lives. The Fair Labor Standards Act limited the number of hours that most laborers could work and set the country's first minimum wage. The Social Security Act of 1935 included three major programs: a fund for retired workers, unemployment insurance for people who lose their jobs, and welfare grants for the poor.

While the New Deal did not end the Great Depression, it greatly lessened its severity. More people had jobs, and federal programs were put into place to help those unable to work. The New Deal programs also set up important government controls over the economy that helped the country better weather later recessions like the one in 2008.

Crisis Comparison

In the fall of 2008, many economists predicted that the economy could fall into a severe recession or even a depression. Some felt the regulations that were put in place during the Great Depression had been seriously weakened over time. They believed, as a result, that the FDIC might not be able to guarantee deposits in the event of a full-scale banking collapse. They pointed out that deregulating the activities of banks and lenders had brought on the credit crisis by undoing some of these economic controls.

Other economists dismissed the idea. During the Great Depression, new policies were put into action to govern the way that banks do business and guarantee that money held by the banks would be insured. Economists felt that these safeguards—along with a broader government relief system than any that existed when the Great Depression began—would protect the economy in this latest crisis. For instance, some banks stepped in to purchase failing banks. Unlike when Herbert Hoover was in office, the government now willingly spends itself into a deficit in order to spur the economy and protect its citizens. Also, governments today are more ready to step in and offer direct aid to individuals and businesses during an economic crisis. For instance, in September 2008, the government took steps to bail out mortgage lenders Fannie Mae and Freddie Mac, as well as insurance giant American International Group (AIG). In early October, the government passed a $700 billion rescue plan to help struggling banks.

Similarly, in late 2008, Barack Obama, who had been elected president but hadn't yet taken office, proposed an economic stimulus and rescue package that involved public works projects, homeowner and taxpayer relief, and assistance to banks, manufacturers, and small businesses. The cost of this large and ambitious plan was estimated to

In 2008, the US government used nearly $200 billion to bail out AIG, a major insurance company.

be as much as $1 trillion. In February 2009, having taken office, President Obama signed this package into law. In these ways, the United States was far more prepared to respond to the 2008–2009 financial crisis.

Thankfully, in the Great Recession and in other smaller recessions that have occurred since the Great Depression, the United States has been better able to recover when the stock market drops and unemployment rises. Given the effective protections and safeguards put into the economy during the Great Depression, the United States has been able to effectively bounce back from periods of contraction. Hopefully, it will continue to do so to avoid any future depressions that remotely resemble the Great Depression.

GLOSSARY

austerity measures Government actions taken to cut spending and increase revenue.

bailout An influx of money meant to rescue a business or country.

bankruptcy A legal process through which an individual or a business declares an inability to repay debt.

consumer price index (CPI) This number represents the average change in the cost of goods or services over a period of time.

credit Confidence in a purchaser's ability and intention to pay, displayed by entrusting the buyer with goods or services without immediate payment.

debt The total amount an individual, business, or country owes another.

deficit The amount by which spending exceeds income or assets within a specific period of time.

deflation A fall in the general price of goods or a contraction of credit and available money.

depression A period during which stock market values, business, and employment decline severely or remain at a very low level of activity; a severe recession.

economy A network of producers, distributors, and consumers of goods and services in a local, regional, national, or global community.

gross domestic product (GDP) The total market value of goods and services produced by workers and capital within a nation's borders during a given period.

gross national product (GNP) The total monetary value of all final goods and services produced by a country during a given year, including goods and services produced by people or companies from that country but operating in a different country.

inflation An increased cost of goods and services often coupled with a decreased value of money.

interest A sum paid or charged for the use of money or for borrowing money, often expressed as a percentage of money borrowed and to be paid back within a given time.

peak The highest point in the business cycle; it marks a turning point when the cycle moves into contraction or a recession.

recession A period of general economic decline, defined usually as a contraction in the GDP for six months or longer.

stock Ownership shares of a particular company or corporation.

subsidy A grant issued by a government to assist a company it considers important to the public that is struggling financially.

tariff A government tax on imports or exports.

trough The lowest point in the business cycle; it marks a turning point when the cycle moves toward expansion and recovery.

FURTHER INFORMATION

Books

Bodden, Valerie. *Federal Reserve System*. Agents of Government. Mankato, MN: The Creative Company: 2015.

Riggs, Kate. *The Great Recession*. Turning Points. Mankato, MN: The Creative Company, 2017.

Saidian, Siyavush. *The Great Depression: Worldwide Economic Crisis*. American History. New York: Lucent Books, 2017.

Strasser, Todd. *No Place*. New York: Simon & Schuster Books for Young Readers, 2015.

Websites

Library of Congress: The Great Depression

http://www.loc.gov/teachers/classroommaterials/themes/great-depression/students.html

On this webpage, the Library of Congress lists several different resources useful to students interested in learning about the Great Depression.

The Library of Economics and Liberty: High School Economic Topics

http://www.econlib.org/library/Topics/HighSchool/HighSchoolTopics.html

This website provides an extensive glossary containing economics terms and definitions.

Videos

The Business Cycle (Economic Expansions and Contractions) Explained in One Minute

https://www.youtube.com/watch?v=VwRJzVEUclA

This brief video provides a quick overview and explanation of the business cycle while also explaining the difference between a depression and a recession.

The 2008 Financial Crisis: Crash Course Economics #12

https://www.youtube.com/watch?v=GPOv72Awo68

This video provides a description of the financial decisions that led to the Great Recession.

Organizations

Board of Governors of the Federal Reserve System

20th Street and Constitution Avenue NW
Washington, DC 20551
(202) 263-4869
Website: http://www.federalreserve.gov

The Federal Reserve System serves as the nation's central bank. Its headquarters are in Washington, DC, and there are twelve Reserve Banks located in major US cities.

Department of Finance Canada

140 O'Connor Street
Ottawa, ON K1A 0G5
Canada
(613) 992-1573

Website: http://www.fin.gc.ca

The Department of Finance Canada oversees the Canadian government's budget and spending.

International Monetary Fund
700 19th Street, NW
Washington, DC 20431
(202) 623-7000
Website: https://www.imf.org/external/index.htm

Established in 1944, the IMF is a specialized agency of that United Nations that promotes international financial stability.

Junior Achievement
1 Education Way
Colorado Springs, CO 80906
(719) 540-8000
Website: https://www.juniorachievement.org/web/ja-usa/home

This organization, which has local chapters throughout the country, is focused on preparing young adults "to succeed in a global economy."

Treasury Board of Canada Secretariat
Strategic Communications and Ministerial Affairs
L'Esplanade Laurier, 9th Floor, East Tower
140 O'Connor Street
Ottawa, ON K1A 0R5
Canada
(877) 636-0656
Website: http://www.tbs-sct.gc.ca

This government body provides oversight of financial management functions in other departments and agencies.

United States Department of the Treasury
1500 Pennsylvania Avenue, NW
Washington, DC 20220
(202) 622-2000
Website: http://www.ustreas.gov

The Department of the Treasury manages the US government's finances, promotes economic growth and stability, and ensures the security of the US and international financial systems.

SELECTED BIBLIOGRAPHY

Alderman, Liz, Larry Buchanan, Eduardo Porter, and Karl Russel. "Is Greece Worse Off Than the US During the Great Depression?" *New York Times*, July 9, 2015. https://www.nytimes.com/interactive/2015/07/09/business/international/is-greece-worse-off-than-the-us-during-the-great-depression.html?mtrref=www.google.com.

Bonner, Bill, and Addison Wiggin. *Empire of Debt: The Rise of an Epic Financial Crisis*. Hoboken, NJ: John Wiley & Sons, Inc., 2006.

DePillis, Lydia. "10 Years After the Financial Crisis, Have We Learned Anything?" CNN, September 13, 2018. https://money.cnn.com/2018/09/13/news/economy/financial-crisis-10-years-later-lehman/index.html.

Flynn, Sean Masaki. *Economics for Dummies*. Hoboken, NJ: John Wiley & Sons, Inc., 2005.

Gottheil, Fred. *Principles of Economics*. 4th ed. Mason, OH: Thomson Publishing, 2005.

Lanigan, Jane, ed. *Economics: Economic Theory*. Vol. 5. Danbury, CT: Grolier Educational, 2000.

Lawson, Alan. *A Commonwealth of Hope: The New Deal Response to Crisis*. Baltimore, MD: The Johns Hopkins University Press, 2006.

Lowenstein, Roger. *Origins of the Crash: The Great Bubble and Its Undoing*. New York: The Penguin Press, 2004.

Nardo, Don, ed. *The Great Depression*. Turning Points in World History. San Diego, CA: Greenhaven Press, Inc., 2000.

"One Hundred Years of Price Change: The Consumer Price Index and the American Inflation Experience." United States Department of Labor: Bureau of Labor Statistics, April 2014. https://www.bls.gov/opub/mlr/2014/article/one-hundred-years-of-price-change-the-consumer-price-index-and-the-american-inflation-experience.htm.

Pisani, Bob. "A Cyberattack Could Trigger the Next Financial Crisis, New Report Says." CNBC.com, September 13, 2018. https://www.cnbc.com/2018/09/13/a-cyberattack-could-trigger-the-next-financial-crisis.html.

Rauchway, Eric. *The Great Depression and the New Deal: A Very Short Introduction*. New York: Oxford University Press, 2008.

Sowell, Thomas. *Basic Economics: A Citizen's Guide to the Economy*. New York: Basic Books, 2000.

INDEX

Page numbers in **boldface** refer to images.

ABOUT THE AUTHOR

Chet'la Sebree is a writer, editor, and researcher. She has written and edited several books for Cavendish Square Publishing, including one on the Great Depression. She has degrees in English and creative writing from the University of Richmond and American University, respectively. She is from the Mid-Atlantic region.